Mastering Strategic Productivity

Unlocking Practical Strategies for Sustainable Success in a Fast-paced World

Hopper Roger

Copyright © [Hopper Roger] [2024]

All rights reserved. No part of this publication may be reproduced, distributed, or transmitted in any form or by any means, including photocopying, recording, or other electronic or mechanical methods, without the prior written permission of the publisher, except in the case of brief quotations embodied in critical reviews and certain other noncommercial uses permitted by copyright law.

TABLE OF CONTENT

Introduction — 5

Chapter 1: Understanding Strategic Productivity — 7

   Definition and Significance — 9

   Exploring the concept of strategic productivity and its relevance in a dynamic environment — 12

Chapter 2: Principles of Effective Prioritization — 14

   Strategies for Effective Prioritization — 16

Chapter 3: Embracing Personal Rhythm — 19

   Strategies to Embrace Personal Rhythm — 20

   Aligning Work with Individual Pace and Preferences — 23

   Strategies to Align Work with Individual Pace and Preferences — 24

Chapter 4: Pursuing Quality Excellence — 27

   Strategies for Achieving Quality Excellence — 30

   Prioritizing excellence over quantity in all endeavors. — 31

Chapter 5: Time Mastery Techniques　　35

Practical Time Mastery Techniques　　37

Efficient time management strategies for enhance productivity　　39

Chapter 6: Overcoming Procrastination　　42

Strategies for overcoming procrastination and increasing productivity　　44

Chapter 7: Distraction Management　　49

Techniques for minimizing distractions and maintaining focus　　50

Chapter 8: Establishing Work-Life Harmony　　52

Chapter 9: Fostering Focus & Creativity　　55

Cultivating Mindfulness and Fostering Innovation for Strategic Productivity　　57

Designing a Productive Environment　　59

Creating an optimal workspace and organizational culture　　62

Conclusion Sustaining Strategic Productivity　　66

Introduction

In today's fast-paced world, when every minute appears to demand our attention, Productivity has grown into a complicated pursuit that goes well beyond just completing tasks. Productivity is no longer just about crossing things off a to-do list or increasing production; it's about developing an intentional and purposeful approach to how we use our time, energy, and resources. In today's fast-paced world, where the change shows no signs of slowing, mastering productivity has become more than a talent, but a must for managing the intricacies of our personal and professional lives.

Enter strategic productivity, a paradigm change that stresses working smarter, not harder. Unlike traditional definitions of productivity, which focus exclusively on efficiency, strategic productivity goes deeper, urging us to consider the importance and influence of our activities in connection to our overall aims and values. It's about making deliberate decisions about where to focus our efforts, ensuring that each activity we do adds significantly to our broader goals. In essence, strategic productivity is about connecting our activities with our aspirations, instilling a feeling of purpose and direction in whatever we do.

Strategic productivity is fundamentally concerned with both the path and the destination. It is about having a mindset of continual improvement and progress, always looking for new methods to streamline and enhance our procedures. In this world, where the demands on our time and attention appear to be limitless, mastering strategic productivity necessitates a willingness to question traditional wisdom, experiment with new ways, and adopt an innovative mindset. It's about understanding that great productivity is more than just doing more; it's about doing better, in a way that reflects our beliefs and objectives.

Chapter 1

Understanding Strategic Productivity

Effectiveness and efficiency are two important pillars of production, with each playing a critical part in generating optimal results. Although they are closely similar, there is a significant difference between the two. Effectiveness refers to doing the right things, whereas efficiency is concerned with executing them correctly.

Consider the scenario of a rail network that has frequent disruptions due to engineering work. Train companies may offer a bus substitute service, but if commuters have lengthier rides and are dissatisfied, it indicates a lack of effectiveness. In such circumstances, seeking alternative solutions, such as finishing engineering tasks faster or scheduling them during off-peak hours, might improve effectiveness by addressing the underlying source of the problem.

Effectiveness ensures that the correct line of action is followed, with activities aligned with broader goals and priorities. However, simply doing the right things isn't enough; they must also be done well. Here's where efficiency comes into play. Efficiency ensures that activities be completed as effectively as possible by streamlining procedures, maximizing resource allocation, and reducing waste.

It's critical to understand that, while effectiveness and efficiency are usually complementary, there may be times when a shift in focus is required. When circumstances make the appropriate course of action impracticable or unfeasible, it is necessary to adapt and prioritize efficiency. This may entail making difficult decisions and considering different techniques to achieving the desired results.

While effectiveness guarantees that tasks are in line with goals, efficiency ensures that they are completed optimally. Both are critical to achieving productivity and success. Individuals and organizations may traverse the complexity of decision-making more successfully and accomplish their desired outcomes if they grasp the difference between effectiveness and efficiency, as well as when to prioritize each.

Definition and Significance

In the ever-changing world of business, where innovation and efficiency reign supreme, the concept of "strategic productivity" develops as a guiding principle that directs businesses toward long-term success. Strategic productivity is fundamentally defined as the seamless integration of strategic management principles with the continuous pursuit of operational excellence. It refers to the intentional alignment of resources, processes, and human capital to achieve set goals and objectives in a way that not only improves performance but also strengthens competitive positioning in the market.

Strategic productivity goes beyond simply measuring output per unit of input; it delves further into the strategic orchestration of these factors in order to achieve long-term sustainability and growth. It comprises a holistic strategy that takes into account not only the quantitative components of productivity, but also the qualitative dimensions, such as innovation, adaptation, and resilience.

Strategic productivity is important because it has the potential to change the competitive landscape and drive long-term growth. Organizations that cultivate a culture of continuous improvement and innovation can improve their operational agility, market responsiveness, and ability to capitalize on emerging possibilities. Furthermore, strategic productivity acts as a driver for organizational alignment, ensuring that all aspects of the business are focused on common strategic goals, thereby increasing synergy and coherence across the corporation.

Strategic productivity is particularly important for increasing organizational resilience and adaptation in the face of disruptions and uncertainty. Organizations can improve their ability to weather market swings, reduce risks, and capitalize on emerging trends by optimizing resource allocation and operational efficiency. Furthermore, strategic productivity enables firms to stand out in the marketplace by providing higher value to customers, encouraging loyalty and competitive advantage.

In essence, strategic productivity is a guiding principle that drives organizational strategy and performance, rather than just an efficiency indicator. It is a strategic requirement for organizations that want to survive in today's hypercompetitive business environment by unlocking untapped potential, fostering innovation, and positioning themselves for long-term success. As businesses traverse the difficulties of today's business climate, strategic productivity emerges as a cornerstone of strategic management, changing organizations' trajectory and propelling them to new heights of success.

Exploring the concept of strategic productivity and its relevance in a dynamic environment

In today's fast-paced, ever-changing world, the concept of productivity has evolved. It is no longer enough to just get things done; it is also necessary to accomplish the right things in the right way in order to generate significant results. Here's where strategic productivity comes into play.

Strategic productivity is fundamentally about effectiveness, not just efficiency. It is about knowing our goals and priorities and coordinating our efforts to attain them. Strategic productivity is critical for success in a dynamic environment where priorities change, resources are limited, and difficulties abound.

Consider navigating a continuously shifting terrain in which every decision matters. In such cases, being productive entails not only working harder or quicker, but also working smarter. It is about making informed decisions, capitalizing on our skills, and using our resources to reach our goals.

In this dynamic world, strategic productivity serves as a compass, guiding us through uncertainty and complexity. It is important to have a clear sense of direction and purpose, even when the path ahead is uncertain. It is about being flexible, agile, and resilient in the face of adversity.

Furthermore, strategic productivity is more than just individual achievement; it also involves teamwork and synergy. It is about combining different abilities and viewpoints to achieve common aims. In a dynamic environment where change is the only constant, teamwork is critical to creativity and progress.

Chapter 2

Principles of Effective Prioritization

A set of guiding principles is at the heart of good prioritization, assisting us in making educated decisions about where to direct our time, energy, and resources. These principles act as a compass, leading us through the numerous tasks and obligations we face on a daily basis.

The fundamental principle of good prioritization is clear goals. Before we can properly prioritize our tasks, we need to have a clear knowledge of our overall goals and priorities. By setting our goals and objectives early, we can ensure that our efforts are focused on what is genuinely important.

The second premise is to judge urgency and importance. Not all tasks are created equal, and it is critical to distinguish between urgent and vital. Urgent jobs require immediate attention, whereas vital tasks support long-term aims and objectives. By determining the urgency and importance of each assignment, we may prioritize them and distribute resources appropriately.

The third principle considers impact and effort. Some chores may have a major impact on our goals while requiring little effort, whilst others may be time-consuming with little consequence. By weighing the potential impact of each activity against the work necessary, we may prioritize projects that provide the best return on investment.

The fourth principle is flexibility and adaptability. Priorities can change, and unanticipated obstacles may occur. It is critical that we stay flexible and adaptable in our approach to priority, eager to change our plans as necessary to fit changing conditions.

By employing these successful prioritization methods, we may confidently and clearly navigate the complexities of our workload. We can direct our efforts toward tasks that correspond with our objectives, optimize our effect, and move us forward.

Strategies for Effective Prioritization

Now that we've established the basic principles of effective prioritization, let's look at some practical techniques for putting them into action in our daily lives. These tactics will allow us to prioritize work with certainty and efficiency, optimizing our progress and productivity.

1. Establish clear goals and objectives: Start by outlining your aims and objectives. What goals do you wish to attain in the short and long term? Having a clear grasp of your priorities allows you to coordinate your responsibilities and focus on what is most important.

2. Use Prioritization Frameworks: To help prioritize tasks, consider using the Eisenhower Matrix, the Pareto Principle (80/20 Rule), or the ABCDE approach. Experiment with many frameworks to find the one that best suits you and your specific circumstances.

3. Determine Urgency and Importance: Rate each assignment according to its urgency and importance. Urgent jobs require immediate attention, whereas important tasks help to achieve long-term goals. Use tools like deadlines, urgency flags, and priority labels to categorize activities.

4. Consider Impact and work: Prioritize projects based on their potential impact vs the work necessary. Focus on high-impact actions that will get you closer to your goals, while minimizing time spent on low-impact activities. To make progress easier, divide major activities into smaller, more manageable chunks.

5. Review and Adjust Priorities Regularly: Because priorities change over time, they must be reviewed and adjusted on a frequent basis. Set aside time at the start or end of each day to reassess your priorities, reprioritize work as necessary, and ensure alignment with your goals and objectives.

6. Practice Time Blocking: Set aside certain time blocks for different sorts of tasks based on their priority and complexity. Schedule precise time intervals for focused work, meetings, email correspondence, and breaks to ensure that vital tasks receive the attention they require while minimizing distractions.

7. Learn to Delegate and Say No: Understand when work can be assigned to others and when it is okay to say no. Delegating duties frees up time and energy for more important activities, while creating boundaries helps prevent overcommitment and burnout.

Implementing these practical tactics will allow you to efficiently prioritize work, make educated judgments about where to direct your efforts, and achieve maximum growth and productivity in your personal and professional endeavors.

Chapter 3

Embracing Personal Rhythm

In our continuous quest of productivity and success, we frequently miss the significance of personal rhythm—a concept based on the natural ebb and flow of our energy and focus throughout the day. Embracing personal rhythm entails understanding and honoring these fundamental rhythms, which allows us to function in harmony with our bodies' natural tendencies rather than against them. In this section, we'll look deeper into the importance of personal rhythm and ways for using it to boost productivity and well-being.

Personal rhythm is not a one-size-fits-all concept; it is as unique as the individual. Some people thrive in the early morning, while others find their stride in the afternoon or evening. Understanding our personal rhythm entails paying attention to our body's signals and determining when we feel the most alert, focused, and productive. Tuning into these natural indications allows us to plan our days in a way that maximizes efficiency and effectiveness.

The benefits of embracing own rhythm go far beyond productivity. Working in harmony with our bodies' natural rhythms allows us to feel more satisfied, fulfilled, and well-balanced. When we schedule our duties and activities around our peak energy hours, work feels less like a chore and more like a worthwhile undertaking. Furthermore, adopting a personal rhythm can help reduce stress, minimize burnout, and promote a better sense of work-life balance by allowing us to prioritize self-care and relaxation.

Strategies to Embrace Personal Rhythm

1. Determine Your Peak Productivity Periods: Take note of when you feel the most motivated and concentrated during the day. Are you a morning person, or do you feel most alive in the afternoon or evening? Once you've determined your peak

production times, plan your day accordingly to capitalize on these periods of increased performance.

2. Optimize Your Environment: Design a workstation that complements your own rhythm and promotes productivity. To improve focus and concentration during high energy periods, make sure there is enough illumination, comfortable sitting, and few distractions. To improve your work environment, try using ergonomic furniture, relaxing colors, and motivating decor.

3. Prioritize chores Wisely: Save your most difficult and critical chores for times when you are at your peak. Task lists, calendars, and productivity apps can be used to prioritize projects based on their urgency, importance, and energy requirements. Break down huge projects into smaller, more achievable chores to keep momentum and avoid overload.

4. Take regular breaks: Take regular pauses during your working to avoid mental tiredness and maintain peak performance. Use pauses to replenish your batteries, whether through physical activity, mindfulness practices, or simply getting away from your desk for some fresh air. Remember that taking breaks is not a sign of weakness; rather, they are necessary for maintaining productivity and well-being over time.

5. Listen to your body: Pay attention to minor signs from your body and mind all day. Take note when your energy levels begin to dwindle or your attention begins to shift. Instead of pushing through exhaustion or distraction, take a break to pause, reset, and refocus. Trust your instincts and alter your actions to accommodate your personal rhythm.

6. Prioritize self-care: Routines that nourish your body, mind, and spirit. Make time in your calendar for activities that revitalize

and replenish your energy reserves, such as exercise, meditation, creative endeavors, or spending time outside. Remember that self-care is not selfish; it is necessary for maintaining balance and vitality in all areas of your life.

Aligning Work with Individual Pace and Preferences

In today's fast-paced, demanding world, striking a balance between productivity and well-being can be difficult. However, by tailoring our work to our particular speed and tastes, we can achieve a more harmonic and gratifying experience. In this section, we'll look at why it's important to align work with individual pace and preferences, as well as practical ways for doing so.

Every person has a distinct set of rhythms, preferences, and work styles that shape how they approach jobs and activities. Some people flourish in fast-paced, dynamic surroundings, while others prefer more measured and organized approaches. Understanding our own pace and preferences entails understanding these underlying characteristics and tailoring our work routines accordingly.

Work that is tailored to an individual's speed and preferences provides numerous personal and professional rewards. When we operate in accordance with our natural cycles and preferences, jobs become less burdensome and more like possibilities for growth and self-expression. Furthermore, aligning work with personal speed and preferences can boost productivity, job satisfaction, and general well-being by lowering stress, increasing motivation, and instilling a sense of autonomy and control.

Strategies to Align Work with Individual Pace and Preferences

1. Communicate with Others: Share your preferences and boundaries with coworkers, managers, and clients. Tell them when

you're most productive, when you prefer to be undisturbed, and what work arrangements best suit your needs. Establishing clear expectations and boundaries can assist to foster a healthy work atmosphere that values individual differences.

2. Personalize Your Workspace: Design your workspace to match your unique preferences and requirements. Create a work atmosphere that boosts productivity and encourages well-being, whether by adding plants for a touch of greenery, altering lighting to decrease eye strain, or adopting ergonomic furniture for comfort.

3. Use Your Time Wisely: Prioritize projects according to their urgency, importance, and alignment with your personal goals and values. To improve your workflow and reduce procrastination, use time management tactics such as time blocking, batching comparable jobs, and setting realistic deadlines.

4. Establish limits: To avoid burnout and maintain a healthy work-life balance, set clear limits between work and leisure time. Set specific work hours, take regular breaks, and turn off work-related gadgets outside of those hours. By making time for rest, relaxation, and rejuvenation, you can refill your energy reserves and return to work with fresh focus and passion.

5. Engage in Self-Reflection: Regularly evaluate your work habits, routines, and outcomes to uncover areas for development and refinement. Consider what tactics are working best for you and what changes may be required to better align your work with your unique pace and preferences. Be willing to explore and adjust as you refine your approach over time.

Chapter 4

Pursuing Quality Excellence

In today's competitive world, pursuing quality excellence has become critical for firms looking to differentiate themselves and provide outstanding value to their customers. Quality excellence entails more than just adhering to norms and regulations; it represents an unwavering dedication to continual improvement, innovation, and exceeding customer expectations. In this section, we'll look at the necessity of seeking quality excellence and offer practical advice on how businesses might attain and sustain it.

Quality excellence refers to a comprehensive approach to quality management that pervades all aspects of a company's activities, from product design and development to customer service and support. At its core, quality excellence is about striving for perfection in all we do, constantly looking for ways to enhance processes, products, and services in order to provide superior value to our consumers. It necessitates a culture of responsibility, transparency, and collaboration in which every person of the business is encouraged to contribute to quality improvement activities.

The pursuit of quality excellence provides numerous benefits to organizations, employees, and customers. Organizations that regularly produce high-quality products and services can improve their reputation, establish customer loyalty, and gain a competitive advantage in the marketplace. Quality excellence also increases efficiency, productivity, and cost savings as firms reduce errors, rework, and waste. A culture of quality excellence encourages pride, engagement, and job satisfaction among employees by encouraging them to take ownership of their work and strive for perfection in everything they do.

Strategies for Achieving Quality Excellence

Quality excellence necessitates a collaborative effort and a systematic strategy. Organizations can use a variety of tactics to promote continuous improvement and maintain high quality standards:

1. Establish Clear Quality Objectives: Develop quantifiable quality objectives that are consistent with company goals and consumer expectations. Establish key performance indicators (KPIs) to monitor success and pinpoint opportunities for improvement.

2. Empower Employees: Create an empowerment culture in which employees are encouraged to take ownership of quality and suggest ways to improve. Provide staff with the necessary training, resources, and support to effectively perform their duties and contribute to quality improvement efforts.

3. Implement Robust Quality Management Systems: To assure consistency, traceability, and responsibility in quality processes, put in place robust quality management systems (QMS) based on international standards such as ISO 9001. Regularly audit and analyze the QMS to find areas for improvement.

4. Use Lean and Six Sigma approaches to streamline operations, remove waste, and reduce variance. Implement continuous improvement programs, such as Kaizen events and process mapping, to drive incremental changes throughout the organization.

5. Actively solicit and listen to consumer feedback to find areas for improvement and respond to customer problems quickly. Use consumer input to promote product innovation and service improvements that meet or exceed customers' expectations.

6. Encourage Innovation and Collaboration: Create an environment in which employees are encouraged to experiment, take risks, and share best practices. Form cross-functional teams to handle quality improvement projects and harness their aggregate knowledge and ideas.

Prioritizing excellence over quantity in all endeavors.

In the vast terrain of production, there is a fundamental element that distinguishes the adept from the exceptional: the art of effective prioritization. Imagine the mind as a big stage, with tasks competing for attention and recognition. The genuine master of prioritization emergcs here, amidst the noise of chores, like a conductor directing a symphony of subtlety and precision.

At its core, effective prioritization is more than just allocating time; it is about identifying significance among the noise, comprehending the subtle dance between urgency and importance. It necessitates a careful balance of foresight and intuition, perfected through attentive cultivation.

This skill is built on the ability to distinguish between what is merely urgent and what is actually necessary. Urgency, while frequently enticing, can be deceptive—a siren's call that detracts from the profound. True prioritization necessitates an unwavering dedication to the pursuit of significant tasks, unaffected by the pull of instant reward.

Furthermore, successful prioritization is an art of both omission and selection. It takes fortitude to face the countless diversions that pervade the modern world, as well as knowledge to distinguish between the trivial and transformative. In the broad tapestry of production, every "yes" is a commitment, and every "no" is a liberation—a intentional decision to devote one's most valuable resource, time, to pursuits of the highest importance.

Prioritization, however, is not a single undertaking; rather, it is a collaborative symphony performed within the context of relationships and duties. It necessitates empathy, comprehension, and a deep awareness for the interconnectivity of human endeavor. The master of prioritizing understands the intrinsic value of collaboration, harnessing others' skills to raise the collective quest of excellence.

Crucially, good prioritization is a dynamic process, not a static ability, that requires constant improvement and adaptation. It takes humility to own flaws, resilience to weather setbacks, and the willingness to embrace change. In the face of uncertainty, the master of prioritization maintains agility, readjusting priorities with grace and poise.

In the history of human achievement, the mark of a real luminary is not the number of activities performed, but the significance of the attempts undertaken. In this quest of importance, the art of efficient prioritization reaches its pinnacle, a monument to the indomitable spirit of human endeavor and the limitless capacity of the human mind.

By mastering the discipline of successful prioritization, we transcend the commonplace and climb to the extraordinary—a realm in which each activity, each attempt, is filled with purpose and significance. It is a trip characterized by the indelible imprint of human ingenuity rather than the passage of time, demonstrating the eternal ability of the human spirit to change the path of history.

Chapter 5

Time Mastery Techniques

In today's fast-paced environment, efficient time management is essential for success. Time management tools enable people to take control of their schedules, prioritize work, and increase productivity. With the ongoing pressures of work, family, and personal responsibilities, time management becomes critical for preserving balance, decreasing stress, and attaining goals. Individuals can improve their overall quality of life by implementing tried-and-true time management practices.

At the foundation of time mastery is the realization that time is a limited and valuable resource. Each day has a set amount of hours, and how we choose to use those hours has a tremendous impact on our productivity, satisfaction, and success. Time mastery approaches give people the tools and strategies they need to make deliberate decisions about how they spend their time, ensuring that they focus on activities that are consistent with their values, goals, and priorities. Whether it's finishing professional duties, spending time with loved ones, pursuing personal interests, or simply relaxing and recharging, efficient time management allows people to make the most of their time.

The advantages of managing time go far beyond enhanced productivity. Effective time management enables people to have more control, focus, and fulfillment in their daily lives. Prioritizing work and creating clear goals might help people feel less overwhelmed and anxious because they know exactly what has to be done and when. Furthermore, by setting aside time for both work and leisure activities, people can strike a better balance between professional responsibilities and personal well-being. Finally, mastering time enables people to live more deliberately, make significant contributions, and achieve better success in all aspects of their life.

Practical Time Mastery Techniques

1. Prioritization and Goal Setting: First, determine your most essential short- and long-term goals and priorities. Break them down into actionable steps and prioritize them according to their importance and urgency. This will allow you to focus your time and energy on activities that are relevant to your objectives and will move you closer to accomplishing them.

2. Time Blocking: Set aside certain blocks of time in your schedule for various jobs and activities. Create specific time periods for concentrated work, meetings, breaks, and personal activities to ensure that you are making progress on your most critical duties while still allowing for rest and leisure.

3. The Pomodoro Technique: Divide your work into intervals of 25 minutes, followed by brief breaks. During each period, concentrate entirely on a single job, known

as a "Pomodoro," without interruption or distraction. This strategy promotes focus and productivity by utilizing the natural patterns of attention and concentration.

4. Use the Eisenhower Matrix to prioritize tasks based on urgency and importance. This will allow you to direct your time and attention toward projects that have the most impact on your goals and objectives.

5. Time Auditing: Monitor how you spend your time throughout the day to uncover patterns, inefficiencies, and areas for improvement. Maintain a careful record of activities and assess how they relate to your goals and priorities. Use this knowledge to improve your time management by making changes to your schedule and routines.

Efficient time management strategies for enhanced productivity

In the thrilling journey of entrepreneurship, the goal of growth frequently takes center stage, luring businesses with promises of expansion and success. However, in the midst of the rush to acquire clients and scale operations, there is a fundamental truth that is sometimes overlooked: choosing excellence above number is the foundation of long-term success.

Consider the following scenario: would you rather have 100 devoted clients who are profoundly passionate about your product, or 1,000 customers who are simply satisfied? The solution becomes clear when we appreciate the long-term worth of loyal customers, who not only increase revenue but also act as brand ambassadors, accelerating growth via unwavering support and enthusiasm.

Indeed, sustaining a loyal customer base necessitates more than just surface transactions; it necessitates an unwavering dedication to providing outstanding quality in every engagement. This devotion pervades all aspects of the organization, from product development and service delivery to customer involvement and beyond. To prioritize quality above number, entrepreneurs must take a comprehensive approach that considers both internal and external aspects of their operations. Here are some strategies to consider.

To begin, it is critical to understand each customer's specific wants and preferences. Startups that invest time and effort in getting to know their customers on a personal level can personalize their offers to meet and surpass their expectations, building profound loyalty and happiness.

Second, assembling an outstanding team is critical. Individuals in the startup's workforce are more than just employees; they are the driving force behind the company's success. Investing in great personnel and cultivating a culture of cooperation, creativity, and perfection enables the team to continually produce outstanding results.

Details are critical to success. Startups can differentiate themselves in a competitive marketplace by paying close attention to the finer elements of product design, service delivery, and customer experience, creating a lasting impression on both customers and competition.

However, accepting brilliance requires making difficult decisions. Startups must be willing to pass up transitory chances in favor of long-term viability. This includes knowing when to say no, allocating resources to projects with the greatest potential for effect, and avoiding the seduction of indiscriminate development.

The route to excellence is one of continuous learning and adaptation. In an ever-changing world, companies must be nimble and responsive, keeping up with industry trends, consumer behaviors, and technical breakthroughs. Startups that embrace a culture of continuous learning and innovation can position themselves as industry leaders, creating significant development and growth.

Chapter 6

Overcoming Procrastination

Procrastination, which is frequently misunderstood as laziness, reveals a complicated maze of psychological complexities that undermine our best intentions and impede productivity. Contrary to common opinion, procrastination is more than just idleness; it is a complex phenomenon rooted in fear, worry, and self-preservation. This chapter looks into the psychology of procrastination, examines its negative consequences, and provides effective techniques for overcoming this ubiquitous impediment and realizing our full potential.

Procrastination is fundamentally a coping mechanism driven by fear and anxiety, not laziness. Many people procrastinate not because they lack ambition or dedication, but to protect themselves. The dread of failing, the pressure of high expectations, and the anxiety of being judged frequently drive people to postpone in order to protect themselves from potential disappointment or criticism. Postponing duties allows people to maintain control over their self-esteem and self-concept while avoiding the perceived fear of failure or incompetence.

Furthermore, procrastination is frequently fueled by incorrect assumptions and rationalizations. Some people claim to perform better under pressure or use the excitement of last-minute deadlines as inspiration. However, these arguments frequently hide the underlying anxiety and stress caused by procrastination. The brief surge of adrenaline from completing a deadline pales in comparison to the long-term effects of chronic procrastination, which include low self-esteem, increased stress, and decreased well-being.

To eliminate procrastination, one must first develop awareness and comprehension of the fundamental causes of this tendency. Awareness is the first step toward transformation, allowing people to recognize self-defeating procrastination habits and uncover the underlying motivations behind their actions. Individuals can build effective techniques to address and overcome procrastination by understanding its underlying causes.

Strategies for overcoming procrastination and increasing productivity

Time management techniques are valuable tools in the fight against procrastination, but they must be used with caution and moderation. Traditional time management tactics provide structure and organization, but they can also generate anxiety and tension, which leads to procrastination. Individuals should instead employ flexible, adaptable strategies that emphasize progress over perfection and encourage constructive behavior.

Motivation is crucial for overcoming procrastination. Individuals can develop a feeling of purpose and fulfillment by linking duties to intrinsic goals and values, overcoming their fear of failure or judgment. Setting personal goals, focusing on intrinsic rewards, and measuring progress with goal-setting charts can all help people stay motivated and committed to overcoming procrastination.

1. Develop Awareness: Identify the psychological processes that drive procrastination, such as fear of failure, perfectionism, or overwhelm. Take time to consider your own inclinations and triggers, finding patterns of avoidance and procrastination. Individuals can build effective techniques for addressing and overcoming procrastination by recognizing its core causes.

2. Use time management techniques: Accept organizational strategies for structuring tasks and managing time efficiently. Begin by creating specific, attainable goals and breaking them down into smaller, concrete tasks. Prioritize projects based on their priority and deadlines, and schedule time accordingly. To increase productivity and focus throughout the day, use tools like

to-do lists, calendars, and time-blocking tactics.

3. Harness Intrinsic passion: To battle procrastination, cultivate a feeling of purpose and intrinsic passion for undertakings. Instead than focusing simply on external rewards or performance measures, set learning-oriented goals that are consistent with personal beliefs and interests. By linking chores to meaningful objectives and personal progress, people can cultivate a positive mentality that fosters productivity and tenacity.

4. Reduce Distractions: Create an environment conducive to concentration by reducing distractions and increasing productivity. Identify typical sources of distraction, such as social media, email notifications, or untidy workplaces, and take preventative measures to reduce their influence. Set boundaries, create designated work places, or use productivity apps to prevent distractions and improve attention.

5. Develop Self-Discipline: Cultivate self-discipline via persistent practice and dedication to your goals. To create productive habits, set clear goals, establish routines, and stick to a timetable. Use time management techniques like the Pomodoro technique or time-blocking to plan work hours and retain accountability. Individuals can overcome procrastination and achieve their goals more successfully by prioritizing tasks and following through on them with discipline.

6. Seek Accountability: Form partnerships or accountability groups to keep yourself accountable for your efforts and offer mutual support. Share goals, deadlines, and progress reports with trustworthy peers, mentors, or coaches to instill a feeling of accountability and encouragement to keep on track. Regular check-ins and collaborative problem-solving can help people overcome hurdles, stay motivated, and celebrate their accomplishments along the road. Individuals can overcome

procrastination by using accountability to develop a more productive and meaningful lifestyle.

Chapter 7

Distraction Management

In today's fast-paced environment, minimizing distractions is critical for staying focused and productive. Distractions can come from a variety of sources, including technology, ambient influences, and internal thoughts. To properly control distractions, a positive work atmosphere is essential. Begin by choosing a peaceful, uncluttered workspace. Use noise-cancelling headphones to block out background noise and reduce distractions. Set limits with technology by turning off unnecessary notifications and utilizing productivity applications to restrict access to distracted websites. Mindfulness techniques, such as deep breathing exercises or meditation, can help people become more aware of their thoughts and emotions, allowing them to better identify and disengage from distractions. By applying these tactics, individuals can establish a distraction-free atmosphere that fosters concentration and productivity.

Techniques for minimizing distractions and maintaining focus

1. Set Clear Goals and Priorities: Identify your objectives and prioritize tasks based on their importance and urgency. Break down major projects into smaller, achievable stages to prevent feeling overwhelmed and to ensure that your efforts lead to meaningful results.

2. Use Time Management Techniques: Use time blocking to set particular time periods for distinct projects, and the Pomodoro Technique to work in focused intervals separated by short breaks. This improves concentration and reduces burnout.

3. Set Technology Boundaries: To reduce digital distractions, turn off non-essential notifications, utilize applications or browser extensions to prevent distracting websites,

and set aside specific times to read emails and texts.

4. Establish a distraction-free environment: Choose a specialized workspace that is free of outside distractions and favorable to focus. Reduce visual clutter and noise, and use technologies like noise-canceling headphones to avoid distractions.

5. Practice Mindfulness and Meditation: Mindfulness techniques help you become more aware of your thoughts and emotions. Deep breathing exercises or meditation can help you maintain a concentrated attitude and improve your ability to notice and control distractions.

6. Establish Boundaries: Communicate your boundaries to coworkers, family members, and friends, and prioritize your own needs and well-being to effectively keep attention and reduce distractions.

Chapter 8

Establishing Work-Life Harmony

In today's fast-paced and linked world, attaining work-life balance has become more important for people who want to preserve their overall well-being while enhancing productivity. Work-life balance entails striking a balance between professional obligations and personal hobbies, ensuring that neither area of life dominates the other. To successfully build work-life balance, individuals can follow many crucial strategies:

1. Establish Clear limits: One of the most important aspects in establishing work-life balance is to set clear limits between work and personal life. This includes establishing precise work hours and committing to refraining from job-related activities during non-working hours. Individuals can set aside time for relaxation, family, and personal hobbies by defining these boundaries.

2. Prioritize Well-Being: Putting self-care and well-being first is critical for achieving work-life balance. This entails setting aside time for activities such as exercise, meditation, hobbies, and quality time with loved ones. Individuals can recharge and revitalize by investing in activities that improve physical, mental, and emotional health, hence increasing overall productivity and enjoyment.

3. Delegate and Outsource: Knowing when to delegate activities or outsource responsibilities can assist reduce the stress of heavy workloads. Delegating properly, whether by assigning tasks to coworkers or outsourcing personal errands and chores, may free up important time for more meaningful activities.

4. Set Realistic Expectations: Having realistic goals and deadlines is critical for managing expectations and avoiding burnouts. Individuals can lessen stress and feel in

control of their duties by setting attainable goals for both work and personal life.

5. Practice Effective Time Management: Using tried-and-true time management practices is essential for increasing productivity and establishing a work-life balance. This includes prioritizing activities, breaking down projects into manageable pieces, and using tools like calendars and to-do lists to keep organized and focused.

6. Communicate Effectively: Open and transparent communication is essential for achieving work-life balance. Individuals should convey their boundaries, requirements, and expectations to their employers, colleagues, and family members. Advocating for flexible work arrangements, such as remote work or flexible hours, can also help to meet personal obligations and improve work-life balance.

Chapter 9

Fostering Focus & Creativity

Nurturing attention and creativity is critical for achieving peak productivity. It is not just about performing chores, but also about generating meaningful outcomes that get us closer to our long-term goals. We may streamline our efforts and increase our impact, both personally and professionally, by tapping into our attention and creativity.

Focus is essential for productivity. It allows us to prioritize work, distribute resources more efficiently, and maintain momentum in the face of obstacles. When we focus our attention on high-priority activities that are linked with our strategic goals, we may make considerable progress while avoiding distractions.

Creativity is also vital for productivity, as it promotes invention and problem-solving. In today's ever-changing landscape, thinking outside the box and coming up with new ideas is critical to keeping ahead. Creativity enables us to create ground-breaking goods, revolutionary business models, and streamline operational processes, opening up new opportunities for growth and success.

Furthermore, practicing mindfulness increases productivity by encouraging clarity, resilience, and adaptability. Mindfulness activities, such as meditation and deep breathing, improve focus while also developing self-awareness and emotional intelligence. Establishing a mindful culture inside organizations enables people to make informed decisions, negotiate uncertainty confidently, and cooperate successfully to achieve common goals.

Finally, merging focus, creativity, and mindfulness establishes the foundation for productivity. By incorporating these aspects into everyday routines and organizational procedures, we may foster innovation, increase productivity, and achieve long-term success. Embracing attention, creativity, and mindfulness helps us reach our full potential, leading to greater fulfillment and prosperity in all aspects of life and work.

Cultivating Mindfulness and Fostering Innovation for Strategic Productivity

In terms of strategic productivity, the combination of mindfulness and creativity emerges as a potent accelerator for success. Individuals and organizations can realize their greatest potential by cultivating mindfulness practices and developing an innovative culture.

Mindfulness is the foundation of strategic productivity, grounding people in the present moment and improving their capacity to focus and make informed judgments. Mindfulness activities including meditation, breathing exercises, and mindful awareness promote mental clarity, emotional resilience, and increased self-awareness. Individuals who incorporate mindfulness into their everyday routines can improve their cognitive processes, reduce stress, and tackle obstacles with a calm and focused mindset. Mindfulness creates a fertile field for invention by encouraging curiosity, experimentation, and open-mindedness. When people are focused on the present moment and free of distractions, they may unleash their creative potential and explore new ideas with clarity and purpose. By promoting mindful thinking and active listening, organizations may tap into their teams' collective wisdom and produce new solutions to complicated situations.

Creating an innovative culture within firms boosts strategic productivity even more. Organizations that embrace a growth mentality and encourage experimentation and risk-taking can stimulate innovation and promote continual progress. Cultivating an atmosphere that supports variety of thought and facilitates cross-team collaboration promotes an innovative culture in which new ideas thrive and revolutionary breakthroughs arise.

Strategic productivity is built on the foundation of mindful leadership, in which leaders demonstrate honesty, empathy, and resilience. Leaders who prioritize self-care and model thoughtful behaviors inspire trust, improve communication, and build a sense of psychological safety in their teams. Mindful leaders help their people embrace change, adjust to ambiguity, and see obstacles as opportunities for growth and creativity.

In essence, mindfulness and creativity are critical components of strategic productivity. Individuals and teams may unleash their creative potential, make significant development, and achieve long-term success in an ever-changing landscape by incorporating mindfulness practices into daily routines and cultivating an innovative culture inside enterprises. Embracing mindfulness and innovation as strategic imperatives opens the door to transformative growth and prosperity in the digital age.

Designing a Productive Environment

The environment in which we work and live is critical to achieving optimal productivity. Designing a productive setting necessitates deliberate judgments and careful considerations that promote focus, creativity, and well-being. From the arrangement of our workstation to the ambiance of our surrounds, everything influences our productivity and performance.

The concept of ergonomics, or the science of improving human performance and well-being in our surroundings, is important to building a productive workplace. This includes ergonomic furniture, lighting, airflow, and acoustics. Individuals can improve their comfort and concentration by designing a workspace that encourages appropriate posture, lowers physical strain, and limits distractions, resulting in enhanced productivity and efficiency.

A productive atmosphere goes beyond physical ergonomics to include psychological and emotional elements. Incorporating biophilic design elements like natural light, vegetation, and vistas of nature can improve mood, reduce stress, and stimulate cognitive performance. Personalizing the workstation with significant furnishings, images, and keepsakes can also develop a sense of belonging and motivation, resulting in a positive work atmosphere that promotes productivity.

The structure and arrangement of the workstation are critical in increasing productivity. Adopting minimalist and decluttering principles can result in a clean and orderly environment that enhances clarity of thought and minimizes mental tiredness. Furthermore, using smart storage solutions and digital organization tools can streamline workflow and reduce distractions, allowing people to concentrate on the task at hand.

When constructing a productive setting, it is important to consider the role of technology and digital distractions. Time-blocking, device-free zones, and digital detoxes can all assist to offset the harmful effects of technology on productivity and mental health. Individuals can regain control of their time and attention by setting boundaries and creating mindful digital usage practices.

Finally, creating a productive environment requires a comprehensive approach that incorporates physical, psychological, and technical components to support optimal performance and well-being. Individuals may reach their greatest potential and succeed in both their personal and professional lives by creating environments that encourage comfort, inspiration, and focus. Whether at a home office, co-working space, or corporate environment, investing in the design of our surrounds may have a significant impact on productivity, creativity, and general quality of life

Creating an optimal workspace and organizational culture

In today's dynamic workplace, the physical environment and organizational culture have a considerable impact on productivity, creativity, and employee satisfaction. Creating an ideal workspace and cultivating a supportive company culture demands purposeful efforts targeted at encouraging cooperation, innovation, and a feeling of purpose among teammates. Organizations can foster an atmosphere in which people flourish and excel by focusing on aspects such as flexibility, diversity, and well-being.

Recognizing employees' different demands and preferences is central to the concept of the perfect workspace. Flexible work arrangements, such as remote work and flexible hours, allow individuals to adjust their work environments to their specific lifestyles and working habits. Furthermore, providing a choice of workplace options—from quiet places for concentrated jobs to collaborative zones for group projects—allows employees to choose the surroundings that best suit their tasks and preferences.

The physical workspace's design is critical to increasing productivity and well-being. Incorporating biophilic design components such as natural light, indoor plants, and access to outside spaces can have a significant impact on employee mood, stress, and cognitive function. Additionally, investing in ergonomic equipment and amenities, such as adjustable workstations and comfy seats, improves physical health and comfort while lowering the risk of occupational injuries and weariness.

To design an ideal physical workspace, cultivating a positive company culture is critical for long-term success. This includes creating clear communication routes, encouraging transparency, and developing a culture of trust and respect. Employees who feel valued, heard, and supported are more likely to participate actively in their jobs and contribute to the organization's goals.

Cultivating a culture of continual learning and development enables people to broaden their skills and knowledge, which promotes innovation and adaptability. Organizations demonstrate their commitment to their workforce's long-term growth and success by investing in professional development opportunities and offering tools for skills development.

Creating an ideal workspace and organizational culture necessitates a complete strategy that considers the physical, psychological, and social aspects of the workplace. Organizations can build a workplace where people feel empowered, motivated, and inspired to perform at their best by putting flexibility, inclusion, and well-being first. Organizations can achieve long-term success in today's competitive environment by investing in both physical space design and organizational culture development.

Conclusion

Sustaining Strategic Productivity

In our research into sustaining strategic productivity, we discovered insights and techniques that can help individuals and organizations achieve long-term success. We began by addressing the issue of productivity aversion among managers, demonstrating how an overemphasis on production can sometimes jeopardize quality and strategy. We demystified productivity by drawing on a diverse theoretical foundation and providing a thorough assessment of resources and alternative methods to productivity leadership.

Understanding the dangers connected with productivity, we highlighted the significance of connecting corporate objectives with value generation. While productivity is important, it is critical to ensure that efforts are focused on creating what customers actually desire. This necessitates a systematic approach to resource allocation and a thorough understanding of corporate goals.

We discussed the importance of strategic productivity, emphasizing how good leadership and clear communication are critical for driving productivity initiatives. Organizations that encourage a culture of continual improvement and innovation can adjust to changing market circumstances while maintaining a competitive advantage.

Decision-making procedures and workforce involvement were also investigated as potential influences on strategic productivity. We explored how constrained rationality might limit decision-makers' options and emphasized the need of employee engagement in increasing productivity and performance.

Furthermore, we investigated the impact of leadership in driving productivity efforts, emphasizing the importance of strong, visionary leadership at all levels of the business. Effective leaders coach and develop their staff, creating a culture of continual progress and innovation.

Performance measurement and assessment were identified as critical components of sustaining strategic productivity, as they provide insights into the efficacy of productivity programs and guide future decisions. Organizations that regularly analyze performance indicators can identify areas for improvement and execute targeted tactics to increase productivity.

To summarize, sustaining strategic productivity necessitates a comprehensive approach that considers corporate culture, leadership, employee engagement, and continuous improvement. In today's dynamic business climate, firms can overcome hurdles and achieve long-term growth by embracing innovation, cultivating an accountability culture, and efficiently employing technology. Let us carry these ideas forward, constantly reevaluating and learning to ensure long-term success and resilience.

Key Takeaways and Actionable Insights for Long-Term Success

1. Adopt Strategic Thinking: Move from a reactive to a proactive mindset, viewing productivity as a strategic priority rather than merely an operational requirement. Understand the interdependence of productivity, quality, and strategy in order to make educated decisions that generate long-term success. Invest in strategic planning processes that link productivity objectives to the organization's overarching vision, mission, and values. Create a culture that encourages strategic thinking at all levels of the business, encouraging people to think critically about how their work fits into larger strategic goals.

2. Align Organizational Goals: Ensure that productivity efforts are in line with the organization's overall objectives and customer needs. Prioritize value development and client happiness to keep a

competitive advantage in the market. Encourage cross-functional collaboration and communication to ensure that productivity efforts are seamlessly integrated across departments and functions. Goals and priorities should be reviewed and realigned on a regular basis to reflect changing market conditions and client expectations.

3. Promote a Culture of Continuous Improvement: Create an environment in which employees are encouraged to seek out innovative solutions and challenge the status quo. Empower teams to find inefficiencies, execute process improvements, and achieve long-term productivity increases. Implement methods and processes for gathering employee input and suggestions, as well as recognizing and rewarding innovative thinking and contributions. Provide training and tools to help with continuous improvement efforts, as well as to encourage an experimenting and failure-learning culture.

4. Invest in Leadership Development: Cultivate strong, visionary leaders who can inspire and drive teams to reach their potential. Provide leadership development and mentoring initiatives to foster a culture of accountability, innovation, and collaboration. Encourage leaders to lead by example, demonstrating the habits and attitudes that promote productivity and high performance. Create a culture of trust and openness in which leaders actively connect with their people, listen to their issues, and offer guidance and assistance.

5. Prioritize staff involvement: Recognize the importance of staff involvement in increasing productivity and performance. Create a supportive work atmosphere in which workers feel respected, empowered, and driven to do their best job. Encourage open communication and feedback while also providing opportunity for professional development. Recognize and recognize employee efforts, and foster an environment

of respect and recognition. Invest in employee well-being activities, like as wellness programmes and work-life balance efforts, to boost overall employee engagement and happiness.

6. Implement Effective Performance Measurement: Set up clear performance metrics and evaluation methods to track success and identify opportunities for improvement. Use data-driven insights to make more informed decisions and generate continual productivity improvements. Regularly evaluate and analyze performance data to detect trends, patterns, and opportunities. Employees should be given clear performance expectations, as well as regular feedback and coaching to help them improve and succeed.

7. Embrace Innovation and Technology: Use emerging technologies and innovation to optimize processes, automate repetitive jobs, and create new opportunities for productivity growth. Stay current with

industry changes and invest in digital solutions that increase efficiency and productivity. Create an innovative and experimental culture in which employees are encouraged to try out new ideas and problem-solving methods. Provide training and assistance to staff to ensure they have the necessary skills and resources to properly use technology.

8. Encourage Work-Life Balance: Recognize the significance of work-life balance for employee well-being and productivity. Encourage flexible work options, cultivate a wellness culture, and provide resources to help employees strike a healthy work-life balance. Develop policies and programs to promote work-life balance, such as flexible scheduling, remote work choices, and paid time off. Lead by example by making work-life balance a priority in your own life and encouraging others to do the same.

9. Foster a Learning Culture: Create a culture of continual learning and development in

which employees are encouraged to gain new skills, adapt to change, and keep current with industry trends. Invest in training programs, information sharing initiatives, and cross-functional collaboration to encourage creativity and agility. Encourage employees to take responsibility for their own learning and development, and offer chances for mentorship, coaching, and peer-to-peer learning. Create a supportive learning atmosphere in which employees feel comfortable taking risks, experimenting, and learning from mistakes.

10. Maintain agility and adaptability in response to changing market conditions, technology breakthroughs, and client preferences. Continuously evaluate strategy, procedures, and goals to guarantee alignment with changing business needs and long-term performance. Encourage an agile and flexible mindset among employees, empowering them to adapt to change and grab new possibilities. Create a culture of resilience and innovation in which obstacles

are perceived as opportunities for growth and improvement. Adopt a continuous improvement approach, in which modest incremental changes result in significant long-term impact.

www.ingramcontent.com/pod-product-compliance
Lightning Source LLC
Chambersburg PA
CBHW050238230526
45470CB00005B/2004